healthy **dishes**

Easy dishes to cook at home

This edition published in 2010
LOVE FOOD is an imprint of Parragon Books Ltd

Parragon
Queen Street House
4 Queen Street
Bath BA1 1HE, UK

ISBN: 978-1-4075-8103-3

Printed in China

Designed by Talking Design
Cover text and introduction by Frances Eames

Notes for the Reader

This book uses imperial, metric, and US cup measurements. Follow the same units of
measurement throughout; do not mix imperial and metric. All spoon measurements are level:
teaspoons are assumed to be 5 ml, and tablespoons are assumed to be 15 ml. Unless otherwise
stated, milk is assumed to be whole, eggs and individual vegetables such as potatoes are
medium, and pepper is freshly ground black pepper.

The times given are an approximate guide only. Preparation times differ according to the
techniques used by different people and the cooking times may also vary from those given as a
result of the type of oven used. Optional ingredients, variations or serving suggestions have not
been included in the calculations.

Recipes using raw or very lightly cooked eggs should be avoided by infants, the elderly, pregnant
women, convalescents, and anyone with a chronic condition. Pregnant and breastfeeding
women are advised to avoid eating peanuts and peanut products. Sufferers from nut allergies
should be aware that some of the ready-prepared ingredients used in the recipes in this book
may contain nuts. Always check the packaging before use.

Contents

introduction

What we consider to be a healthy meal these days is very different from what earlier generations have believed to be healthy. There was a time, for example, when a meatless meal was considered to be deficient in essential nutrients, and high-fat fried foods were a staple of everyday life.

Nowadays we know that there is nothing wrong with a healthy vegetarian diet, and that too many high-fat fried foods can raise our cholesterol levels and increase our risk of having a heart attack. We are a lot more aware about the health implications of what we eat, and we have never been so well informed. In fact, there is such a wealth of information out there, from the internet, radio and television, magazines and books, that it is easy to feel overloaded, and unable to distinguish between ideas that turn out to be fads of the moment, and solid, practical ideas that are grounded in sound principles of health and nutrition.

Essential steps to a healthy diet

A healthy diet should have a good supply of the following basic food groups:

- Carbohydrates—these are composed of starches and sugars and fall into two categories: simple carbohydrates, which are broken down quickly in the body, and complex carbohydrates, which are broken down more slowly and are therefore a longer-lasting energy source for the body. You should therefore try to eat more complex carbohydrates, such as whole wheat bread, whole wheat pasta, and brown rice, and limit your intake of the simple carbohydrates, found in cakes, candies, and other sugary foods.

- Fats—not all fats are bad. Polyunsaturated fats, found in oily fish and soybean oil, and mono-unsaturated fats, found in olive oil and peanut oil, are actually good for you. The ones to limit are the saturated fats—these are the ones that tend to clog your arteries, and can be found in foods such as meat and dairy products. You should restrict saturated fats to around 10 percent of your daily food intake.

- Protein—this is essential for the body's growth and development, and can be found in meat, poultry, fish, dairy products, eggs, soybeans and other beans, and nuts.

Other things you should do to ensure a healthy diet include:

- Drink plenty of water—this helps to carry nutrients around the body, aids good digestion, and helps to cleanse and hydrate the body. You should aim to drink around 8 cups of water a day, but don't overdo it because this can actually create its own problems for your health.

- Limit alcohol intake to 1 drink a day if you are a woman, and 2 drinks a day if you are a man. A standard drink is defined as 12 ounces of beer, 8 ounces of malt liquor, 5 ounces of wine, or 1.5 ounces of distilled liquor.

- Restrict your intake of caffeine, which is found, for example, in coffee, tea, and soda.

Experts also recommend that you eat 5–7 portions of fruit and vegetables a day. Fruit juice counts as one portion, no matter how much you drink, and starchy vegetables such as potatoes don't count.

Creating healthy dishes

If you keep the above points in mind whenever you are preparing and cooking food, you should find your dishes are usually naturally healthy. In addition, choose fresh, natural ingredients wherever possible, and keep any fat and salt to a minimum. Steam vegetables instead of bringing them to a boil in order to retain as many of their nutrients as possible. Try switching to lower-fat versions of ingredients where available. For example, use light cream or low-fat yogurt instead of heavy cream, and full-fat yogurt.

Essential equipment

You don't need lots of special equipment to prepare and cook healthy dishes—the usual basic kitchen items will get you started. In addition, however, it would be worth investing in some nonstick pots and pans, especially a skillet, so that you can cut down on the amount of fat you use for cooking, and you will find a wok ideal for cooking low-fat, healthy stir-fries.

boosting breakfasts

Breakfast
Smoothie

SERVES 2

1 cup orange juice

½ cup plain yogurt

2 eggs

2 bananas, sliced and frozen

whole bananas, or slices of banana,
    to decorate

Pour the orange juice and yogurt into a food processor or blender and process gently until combined.

Add the eggs and frozen bananas and process until smooth.

Pour the mixture into glasses and decorate the rims with whole bananas or slices of banana. Serve.

Calories: 272   Fat: 9g   Sat Fat: 3g   Salt: 0.4g

Detox
Special

SERVES 2

1 mango

4 kiwi fruit

1½ cups pineapple juice

4 fresh mint leaves

Cut the mango into 2 thick slices as close to the pit as possible. Scoop out the flesh and chop coarsely. Cut off any flesh adhering to the pit. Peel the kiwi fruit with a sharp knife and chop the flesh.

Put the mango, kiwi fruit, pineapple juice, and mint leaves into a food processor or blender and process until thoroughly combined. Pour into chilled glasses and serve.

Calories: 173   Fat: 1g   Sat Fat: 0g   Salt: 0.5g

Mango, Lime &
Lemongrass Zinger

SERVES 4

⅓ cup freshly squeezed lime juice

1 oz/25 g lemongrass, plus 2 extra
  stalks, peeled and halved,
  to garnish

1 small very ripe mango

3 cups low-calorie tonic water

8 ice cubes, to serve

Pour the lime juice into a glass bowl.

Remove the outer brown part of the lemongrass and discard. Finely shred the remaining parts and add to the lime juice.

Cut lengthwise through the mango either side of the flat central pit. Cut away the flesh from around the pit and peel. Coarsely chop the flesh and add to the bowl.

Using a handheld electric blender, blend until the mango is smooth, or use a food processor. Cover the bowl with plastic wrap and refrigerate for at least 2 hours before passing through a fine strainer.

Put a couple of ice cubes each into 4 glasses, divide the mango puree between the glasses, and top off with tonic water. Add a halved lemongrass stalk to each glass to use as a stirrer.

Calories: 23   Fat: 1g   Sat Fat: 0.0g   Salt: 0.0g

Spiced Whole Wheat Muffins
with Marmalade & Raspberry Yogurt

SERVES 6

canola or vegetable oil spray

scant 1 cup all-purpose flour

½ tsp baking powder

scant ½ cup whole wheat flour

½ tsp ground allspice

1 tbsp canola or vegetable oil

1 egg, lightly beaten

⅔ cup buttermilk

1 tsp grated orange zest

1 tbsp freshly squeezed orange juice

1 tsp low-sugar marmalade,
 for glazing

Filling

generous ⅓ cup 0% fat strained
 plain yogurt

1 tsp low-sugar marmalade

½ tsp grated orange zest

scant ½ cup fresh raspberries

Preheat the oven to 325°F/160°C. Spray a six-hole muffin pan lightly with oil.

Sift the all-purpose flour with the baking powder into a large mixing bowl. Using a fork, stir in the whole wheat flour and allspice until thoroughly mixed. Pour in the oil and rub into the flour mixture with your fingertips. In a separate bowl, mix the egg, buttermilk, and orange zest and juice together, then pour into the center of the flour mixture and mix with a metal spoon, being careful not to overmix—the batter should look a little uneven and lumpy.

Spoon the batter into the prepared pan to come about three quarters of the way up the sides of each hole. Bake in the oven for 30 minutes, or until golden brown and a skewer inserted into the center of a muffin comes out clean. Remove from the oven and transfer to a wire rack. Brush with the marmalade and let cool.

For the filling, mix the yogurt with the marmalade and orange zest. Cut the warm muffins through the center and fill with the yogurt mixture and raspberries.

Calories: 150   Fat: 3.5g   Sat Fat: 0.5g   Salt: 0.2g

Melon & Strawberry
Crunch

SERVES 4

⅓ cup rolled oats

¼ cup oat bran

2 tbsp toasted slivered almonds

scant ¼ cup plumped dried apricots,
  finely chopped

½ melon, such as Galia

8 oz/225 g strawberries

⅔ cup low-fat milk or orange juice,
  to serve (optional)

Put the rolled oats and oat bran in a bowl and stir in the almonds and dried apricots.

Discard the skin and seeds from the melon and cut into small bite-size pieces. Halve the strawberries if large.

Divide the rolled oat mixture among 4 individual bowls then top with the fruits. Serve with low-fat milk.

| Calories: 142 | Fat: 5g | Sat Fat: 0.5g | Salt: 0.8g |

Fruity
Yogurt Cups

SERVES 4

2 cups low-fat plain yogurt

1½ tbsp finely grated orange rind

8 oz/225 g mixed berries, such as
  blueberries, raspberries, and
  strawberries, plus extra to decorate

fresh mint sprigs, to decorate
  (optional)

Set the freezer to rapid freeze at least 2 hours before freezing this dish. Line a 12-hole muffin pan with 12 paper cake cases, or use small ramekin dishes placed on a baking sheet.

Mix the yogurt and orange rind together in a large bowl. Cut any large strawberries into pieces so that they are the same size as the blueberries and raspberries.

Add the fruit to the yogurt then spoon into the paper cases or ramekins. Freeze for 2 hours, or until just frozen. Decorate with extra fruit and mint sprigs, if using, and serve. Remember to return the freezer to its original setting afterward.

Calories: 80   Fat: 1g   Sat Fat: 0.7g   Salt: 0.2g

Bircher
Granola

SERVES 4

3 cups rolled oats

1 tbsp wheat germ

scant 1 cup whole milk or soymilk

2 tbsp honey, plus extra for serving
(optional)

2 tbsp plain yogurt

1 apple, peeled, cored, and grated

1 cup chopped nuts, such as
macadamia nuts, cashews,
or hazelnuts

mixed berries, such as blueberries,
raspberries, and strawberries

fruit puree, to serve (optional)

The night before serving, mix the oats, wheat germ, and milk together in a bowl, cover with plastic wrap, and let chill overnight.

To serve, stir the oat mixture, add the honey, yogurt, and apple, and mix well.

Spoon into serving bowls, top with the nuts and berries, and drizzle over a little more honey, or fruit puree, if using.

| Calories: 391 | Fat: 22g | Sat Fat: 5g | Salt: 0.1g |

light
lunches

Chunky Vegetable
Soup

SERVES 6

2 carrots, sliced

1 onion, diced

1 garlic clove, crushed

12 oz/350 g new potatoes, diced

2 celery stalks, sliced

4 oz/115 g closed-cup mushrooms, quartered

14 oz/400 g canned chopped tomatoes in tomato juice

2½ cups vegetable stock

1 bay leaf

1 tsp dried mixed herbs or 1 tbsp chopped fresh mixed herbs

½ cup corn kernels, frozen or canned, drained

2 oz/55 g green cabbage, shredded

freshly ground black pepper

few sprigs of fresh basil, to garnish (optional)

crusty whole wheat rolls, to serve

Put the carrots, onion, garlic, potatoes, celery, mushrooms, tomatoes, and stock into a large pan. Stir in the bay leaf and herbs. Bring to a boil, then reduce the heat, cover, and let simmer for 25 minutes.

Add the corn and cabbage and return to a boil. Reduce the heat, cover, and let simmer for 5 minutes, or until the vegetables are tender. Remove and discard the bay leaf. Season to taste with pepper.

Ladle into warmed soup bowls and garnish with basil. Serve at once with whole wheat rolls.

Calories: 100   Fat: 0.7g   Sat Fat: 0.1g   Salt: 0.3g

Creamy Lima Bean,
Porcini & Tarragon Soup

SERVES 4

2½ oz/70 g leek (white part only),
    cut into ½-inch/1-cm cubes

3½ oz/100 g peeled weight, onion,
    cut into ½-inch/1-cm cubes

2½ oz/70 g celery, cut into ½-inch/
    1-cm cubes

1 garlic clove, peeled and crushed

2 bay leaves

5½ oz/150 g fresh open-cap
    mushrooms, cut into ½-inch/
    1-cm cubes, plus 2 tbsp diced to
    garnish

⅛ cup dried porcini mushrooms,
    soaked in ¼ cup hot water and
    drained

3 oz/85 g peeled weight, potato,
    cut into ½-inch/1-cm cubes

4 oz/115 g canned lima beans,
    drained and rinsed under cold
    water

3 cups vegetable stock

1 tbsp chopped fresh tarragon,
    plus extra to garnish

½ cup skim milk

Garnish

2 tsp lemon juice

1½ tsp sugar

pinch of pepper

3 tbsp 0% fat sour cream

Put the leek, onion, celery, and garlic into a large pan over high heat and cook, stirring constantly, for 5 minutes, or until softened but not colored. You will not need any oil as the steam and the continuous stirring will prevent the vegetables from sticking.

Add the bay leaves, mushrooms, potato, beans, stock, and tarragon, stir well, and bring to a boil. Reduce the heat, cover, and let simmer for 20 minutes, or until the vegetables are mushy.

Meanwhile, for the garnish, mix the lemon juice, sugar, and pepper together in a separate pan. Add the diced mushroom, cover, and cook over high heat for 4–5 minutes. Remove from the heat and let cool in the pan.

Remove the bay leaves from the soup and discard. Using a handheld electric blender, blend the soup until smooth, or use a food processor. Stir in the milk. Pass through a medium strainer into a serving dish.

To serve, pour the mushroom garnish into the soup, sprinkle over a little tarragon, and add a swirl of sour cream.

Calories: 97   Fat: 0.8g   Sat Fat: 0.1g   Salt: 0.5 g

Green Bean & Walnut
Salad

SERVES 2

1 lb/450 g green beans

1 small onion, finely chopped

1 garlic clove, chopped

4 tbsp freshly grated Parmesan
cheese

2 tbsp chopped walnuts or almonds,
to garnish

Dressing

6 tbsp olive oil

2 tbsp white wine vinegar

salt and pepper

2 tsp chopped fresh tarragon

Trim the beans, but leave them whole. Cook for 3–4 minutes in salted boiling water. Drain well, refresh under cold running water, and drain again. Put into a mixing bowl and add the onion, garlic, and cheese.

Place the dressing ingredients in a jar with a screw-top lid. Shake well. Pour the dressing over the salad and toss gently to coat. Cover with plastic wrap and chill for at least 30 minutes. Remove the beans from the refrigerator 10 minutes before serving. Give them a quick stir and transfer to attractive serving dishes.

Toast the nuts in a dry skillet over medium heat for 2 minutes, or until they begin to brown. Sprinkle the toasted nuts over the beans to garnish before serving.

Calories: 290   Fat: 26.5g   Sat Fat: 6g   Salt: 0.3g

Lentil & Goat Cheese
Salad

SERVES 1

scant ¼ cup dried Puy lentils

1 bay leaf

2 scallions, trimmed and finely
  chopped

1¾ oz/50 g red bell pepper, diced

1 tbsp chopped fresh parsley

3½ oz/100 g cherry tomatoes,
  sliced in half

1¾ oz/50 g arugula

1¼ oz/35 g goat cheese, sliced or
  crumbled

Dressing

1 tsp olive oil

1 tsp balsamic vinegar

½ tsp runny honey

1 garlic clove, peeled and crushed or
  finely chopped

Rinse the lentils and put in a medium-size pan. Add the bay leaf and cover with plenty of cold water. Bring to a boil, then reduce the heat and simmer for 20–30 minutes, or until the lentils are tender. Remove the bay leaf.

Drain the lentils and transfer to a bowl. Add the scallions, bell pepper, parsley, and cherry tomatoes. Mix well.

Whisk together the oil, vinegar, honey, and garlic and stir into the lentils. Serve on a bed of arugula, with the goat cheese sprinkled over.

| Calories: 334 | Fat: 14g | Sat Fat: 7g | Salt: 0.6g |

Smoked Salmon &Wild
Arugula Salad

SERVES 4

1¾ oz/50 g wild arugula leaves

1 tbsp chopped fresh flat-leaf parsley

2 scallions, finely diced

2 large avocados

1 tbsp lemon juice

9 oz/250 g smoked salmon

Dressing

⅔ cup mayonnaise

2 tbsp lime juice

finely grated rind of 1 lime

1 tbsp chopped fresh flat-leaf parsley,
    plus extra sprigs to garnish

Shred the arugula and arrange in 4 individual glass bowls. Sprinkle over the chopped parsley and scallions.

Halve, peel, and pit the avocados and cut into thin slices or small chunks. Brush with the lemon juice to prevent discoloration, then divide among the bowls. Mix together gently. Cut the smoked salmon into strips and sprinkle over the top.

Put the mayonnaise in a bowl, then add the lime juice, lime rind, and chopped parsley. Mix together well. Spoon some of the mayonnaise dressing on top of each salad and garnish with parsley sprigs.

Calories: 506   Fat: 47g   Sat Fat: 8g   Salt: 1g

Chinese Vegetables &
Beansprouts with Noodles

SERVES 4

5 cups vegetable stock

1 garlic clove, crushed

½-inch/1-cm piece fresh ginger,
   finely chopped

8 oz/225 g dried medium egg noodles

1 red bell pepper, seeded and sliced

¾ cup frozen peas

4 oz/115 g broccoli florets

3 oz/85 g shiitake mushrooms, sliced

2 tbsp sesame seeds

8 oz/225 g canned water chestnuts,
   drained and halved

8 oz/225 g canned bamboo shoots,
   drained

10 oz/280 g Napa cabbage, sliced

scant 1 cup bean sprouts

3 scallions, sliced

1 tbsp dark soy sauce

freshly ground black pepper

Bring the stock, garlic, and ginger to a boil in a large pan. Stir in the noodles, red bell pepper, peas, broccoli, and mushrooms and return to a boil. Reduce the heat, cover, and let simmer for 5–6 minutes, or until the noodles are tender.

Meanwhile, preheat the broiler to medium. Spread the sesame seeds out in a single layer on a baking sheet and toast under the preheated broiler, turning to brown evenly—watch constantly because they brown very quickly. Tip the sesame seeds into a small dish and set aside.

Once the noodles are tender, add the water chestnuts, bamboo shoots, Napa cabbage, bean sprouts, and scallions to the pan. Return the stock to a boil, stir to mix the ingredients, and let simmer for an additional 2–3 minutes to heat through thoroughly.

Carefully drain off 1¼ cups of the stock into a small heatproof pitcher and set aside. Drain and discard any remaining stock and turn the noodles and vegetables into a warmed serving dish. Quickly mix the soy sauce with the reserved stock and pour over the noodles and vegetables. Season to taste with pepper and serve at once.

| Calories: 353 | Fat: 9.8g | Sat Fat: 4g | Salt: 2.3g |

slimming suppers

Tofu & Vegetable Stir-Fry
with Rice Noodles

SERVES 1

3½ oz/100 g firm tofu

1¾ oz/50 g dried rice noodles

1 tsp vegetable oil

1¾ oz/50 g bok choy, coarsely
  chopped

1¾ oz/50 g broccoli florets, coarsely
  chopped

1 small carrot, peeled and cut into
  thin strips

⅓ cup bean sprouts

1 tsp vegetarian Thai green curry
  paste

2 tbsp vegetable stock

2 scallions, trimmed and halved
  lengthwise

Marinade

1 tsp soy sauce

1 tbsp lime juice

1 tsp chopped garlic

1 tsp chopped lemongrass

1 tsp chopped fresh ginger

1 tsp chopped fresh red chile

Put the tofu in a shallow dish. Whisk together the soy sauce and lime juice and pour over the tofu with the other marinade ingredients. If possible, let marinate for at least 2 hours.

Cook the noodles according to the package directions. Drain and keep warm.

Heat the oil in a nonstick wok or large skillet. Remove the tofu from the marinade, reserving the marinade, and stir-fry the tofu for 1 minute. Add the bok choy, broccoli, carrot, and bean sprouts and cook, stirring, for an additional 1 minute.

In a small bowl or cup, mix the curry paste, stock, and reserved marinade together. Add half to the stir-fry mixture and cook for an additional 2 minutes.

Add the remaining paste and marinade mix and the scallions to the stir-fry and cook for 1 minute, or until the vegetables are just tender. Serve on a bed of warm noodles.

Calories: 280   Fat: 5g   Sat Fat: 0.5g   Salt: 1.1g

Lentil
Bolognaise

SERVES 4

1 tsp canola or vegetable oil

1 tsp crushed garlic

1 oz/25 g onion, finely chopped

1 oz/25 g leek, finely chopped

1 oz/25 g celery, finely chopped

1 oz/25 g seeded green bell pepper,
  finely chopped

1 oz/25 g, peeled weight, carrot,
  finely chopped

1 oz/25 g zucchini, finely chopped

3 oz/85 g flat mushrooms, diced

4 tbsp red wine

pinch of dried thyme

14 oz/400 g canned tomatoes,
  chopped, strained through a
  colander, and the juice and pulp
  reserved separately

4 tbsp dried Puy (French green)
  lentils, cooked

pepper, to taste

5 oz/140 g dried spaghetti

2 tsp lemon juice

1 tsp sugar

3 tbsp chopped fresh basil, plus extra
  sprigs to garnish

Heat a pan over low heat, add the oil and garlic, and cook, stirring, until golden brown. Add all the vegetables, except the mushrooms, increase the heat to medium, and cook, stirring occasionally, for 10–12 minutes, or until softened and there is no liquid from the vegetables left in the pan. Add the mushrooms.

Increase the heat to high, add the wine, and cook for 2 minutes. Add the thyme and juice from the tomatoes and cook until reduced by half.

Add the lentils and pepper, stir in the tomatoes, and cook for an additional 3–4 minutes.

Meanwhile, cook the spaghetti according to the instructions on the package.

Remove the pan from the heat and stir in the lemon juice, sugar, and basil.

Serve the sauce with the cooked spaghetti, garnished with basil sprigs.

Calories: 210   Fat: 2g   Sat Fat: 0.2g   Salt: 0.2g

Mediterranean Vegetables
with Goat Cheese & Penne

SERVES 1

scant ½ cup dried penne pasta

1 small red bell pepper, seeded and
  cut into bite-size chunks

1 small zucchini, trimmed and cut
  into bite-size slices

1 small red onion, peeled and cut
  into wedges

1 tsp olive oil

pepper, to taste

12 cherry tomatoes, halved

3 pitted black olives, halved

1¼ oz/35 g goat cheese, crumbled

few fresh basil leaves, to garnish

Dressing

2 tsp balsamic vinegar

1 tsp lemon juice

1 tsp torn fresh basil leaves

Put a pan of water on to boil and preheat the broiler to medium–high. Cook the pasta according to the package instructions.

Arrange the bell pepper, zucchini, and onion on a nonstick baking sheet, then brush with the oil and season to taste with pepper. Broil for about 5 minutes. Turn the pieces and continue broiling for an additional 5 minutes, or until tender.

When the pasta is cooked, drain well and transfer to a serving bowl. Stir in the cherry tomatoes, olives, and the charbroiled vegetables with their oil and juices.

Beat together the dressing ingredients and stir into the pasta. Crumble over the goat cheese, then garnish with basil and serve.

Calories: 423   Fat: 16g   Sat Fat: 7g   Salt: 0.8g

Braised Lamb
with Pea Salsa & Quinoa Tabbouleh

SERVES 4

4 x 2¼ oz/60 g leg of lamb steaks,
    all visible fat removed
1¾ oz/50 g onion, finely chopped
1 garlic clove, peeled and crushed
2 bay leaves
2 sprigs of rosemary
generous ⅓ cup water
2 tbsp red wine
generous 1 cup strained canned
    tomatoes

Pea Salsa

1½ oz/40 g green beans, cut into
    ¼-inch/5-mm pieces
1½ oz/40 g shelled peas
1½ oz/40 g sugar snap peas, cut into
    ¼-inch/5-mm pieces
1½ oz/40 g snow peas, cut into
    ¼-inch/5-mm pieces
2 tbsp balsamic vinegar
½ tsp Dijon mustard

Quinoa Tabbouleh

2½ cups water
generous ⅓ cup, dry weight, quinoa
scant ⅓ cup, dry weight, bulgur
    wheat
1 tsp ready-made mint sauce
1 tbsp lemon juice
1¾ oz/50 g tomato, peeled, seeded
    and cut into ¼-inch/5-mm pieces

Preheat the oven to 350°F/180°C. Using a rolling pin or mallet, gently beat the lamb steaks between 2 layers of plastic wrap to ⅟16 inch/ 2 mm thick, then roll up to form olives, folding in the ends to neaten. Heat an ovenproof casserole dish over medium heat, add the onion, garlic, bay leaves, and rosemary and cook until the onion is softened. Add the water, wine, and strained canned tomatoes, then lay the olives on top and bring to a boil. Cover and cook in the oven for 45 minutes, or until the meat is tender.

Meanwhile, to make the salsa, blanch the vegetables, refresh in cold water until cold, and drain. Mix the vinegar and mustard together in a microwaveproof container, add the vegetables, and toss to coat.

To make the tabbouleh, bring the water to a boil in a pan, add the quinoa and bulgur wheat and cook for 12 minutes. Drain, tip into a separate microwaveproof container with the mint sauce, lemon juice, and tomato, and mix well.

Remove the olives from the casserole with a slotted spoon and keep warm. Reduce the sauce over medium heat until thick and syrupy.

Reheat the tabbouleh and salsa in a microwave oven on full power for 1½ minutes. Put the olives on top of the tabbouleh, pour over the sauce, and serve with the salsa.

| Calories: 200 | Fat: 4g | Sat Fat: 1.5g | Salt: 0.4g |

Chicken Sesame
Kebabs

SERVES 2

4 oz/115 g skinless, boneless chicken
   breast, cut into thin strips,
   or chicken stir-fry strips

3 tbsp lemon juice

1½ tbsp soy sauce

1 tsp honey

6 oz/175 g assorted salad greens

1 red onion, thinly sliced

1 large carrot, peeled and grated

1 chicory head (optional)

bunch of radishes, trimmed, washed,
   and sliced

1 tbsp sesame seeds

3 tbsp lowfat plain yogurt

Thread the chicken onto 4 presoaked wooden skewers.

Mix 2 tablespoons of lemon juice, 1 tablespoon of soy sauce, and the honey together in a small bowl. Brush the mixture over the chicken and let marinate for at least 15 minutes.

Preheat the broiler to high and line the broiler rack with foil. Arrange the salad greens on a large serving platter and top with the sliced onion and grated carrot. Divide the chicory into separate leaves, if using, and place around the edge of the platter. Scatter over the radishes.

Cook the chicken kebabs under the broiler for 8–10 minutes or until the chicken is thoroughly cooked. Remove from the broiler and sprinkle with the sesame seeds.

Mix the yogurt, the remaining lemon juice, and soy sauce in a small bowl and drizzle over the salad. Serve 2 kebabs per portion.

Calories: 100   Fat: 4g   Sat Fat: 1g   Salt: 0.8g

Thai Crab
Cakes

SERVES 6

10½ oz/300 g canned crabmeat, drained

1–2 fresh Thai chiles, seeded and finely chopped

6 scallions, trimmed and thinly sliced

5 oz/140 g zucchini, grated

4 oz/115 g carrot, peeled and grated

1 tbsp chopped fresh cilantro

2 tbsp cornstarch

2 egg whites

1 spray sunflower oil

Dipping sauce

⅔ cup lowfat plain yogurt

Tabasco sauce, to taste

2 tsp sesame seeds

lime wedges, to garnish

Place the crabmeat in a bowl and stir in the chiles, scallions, grated zucchini, and carrot with the chopped cilantro. Add the cornstarch and mix well.

Beat the egg whites together in a separate bowl then stir into the crab mixture and mix together.

Lightly spray a nonstick skillet with the oil then drop small spoonfuls of the crab mixture into the skillet. Pan-fry the crab cakes over low heat for 3–4 minutes, pressing down with the back of a spatula. Turn over halfway through cooking. Cook the crab cakes in batches.

For the sauce, mix the yogurt and Tabasco sauce, to taste, in a small bowl and stir in the sesame seeds. Spoon into a small bowl and use as a dipping sauce with the cooked crab cakes. Serve garnished with lime wedges.

| Calories: 120 | Fat: 4.5g | Sat Fat: 0.6g | Salt: 0.6g |

dainty desserts

Strawberry & Orange
Delight

SERVES 2

1¾ cups orange juice

1 tbsp gelatin, or vegetarian
   equivalent (gelozone)

3¼ oz/90 g small strawberries, sliced

Put scant ½ cup of the juice in a small heatproof bowl, then sprinkle over the gelatin and let stand for 5 minutes. Place the bowl over a pan of simmering water and stir until the gelatin melts and the liquid becomes clear, then stir in the remaining juice.

Divide the strawberries between 2 serving dishes. Pour over enough juice to just cover the strawberries, then transfer to the refrigerator for 30 minutes, or until set.

Pour in the remaining juice and return to the refrigerator until set.

Calories: 85   Fat: 0g   Sat Fat: 0g   Salt: 0g

Fresh Fruit
Wedges

SERVES 10

sunflower oil, for oiling

2 eggs

heaping ¼ cup superfine sugar

1 tbsp finely grated lemon rind

scant ½ cup self-rising flour, sifted

1 tbsp freshly squeezed lemon juice,
    strained

Filling and Decoration

12 oz/350 g ripe plums or other fruits
    of your choice

1 cup low-fat plain set yogurt

1 tsp confectioners' sugar, sifted

Preheat the oven to 425°F/220°C. Lightly oil and base line a 9-inch/23-cm cake pan with nonstick parchment paper.

Break the eggs into a heatproof bowl and add the superfine sugar and lemon rind. Place the bowl over a pan of gently simmering water and whisk until the whisk leaves a trail when it is dragged lightly across the surface. Remove from the heat and whisk until cool.

Add the flour to the bowl and stir very lightly into the whisked batter, taking care not to overmix. Add the lemon juice and stir lightly then pour into the prepared pan. Tap lightly on the counter to remove any air bubbles.

Bake for 8–10 minutes, or until the top springs back lightly when touched. Remove from the oven and let cool for 10 minutes before turning out, discarding the lining paper.

Halve the plums, discard the pits, and slice.

Place the sponge cake on a serving plate and spoon the yogurt on top. Arrange the plums over. Sprinkle with the sifted confectioners' sugar and serve cut into 10 wedges.

| Calories: 100 | Fat: 1.8g | Sat Fat: 0.5g | Salt: 0.2g |

Steamed Spiced Exotic
Fruits

SERVES 4

2 kiwifruit, peeled and halved

4 rambutan or litchis, peeled, halved, and pitted

2 passion fruit, flesh scooped out

8 Cape gooseberries, papery leaves removed and fruit halved

3 oz/85 g mango, peeled weight, cut into ¾-inch/2-cm cubes

1 persimmon, cut into ¾-inch/2-cm slices

⅜ cup fresh raspberries

2 vanilla beans, split in half lengthwise

2 cinnamon sticks, broken in half

4 star anise

4 fresh bay leaves

4 tbsp freshly squeezed orange juice

Preheat the oven to 400°F/200°C.

Cut four 16 x 16-inch/40 x 40-cm squares of parchment paper and four foil squares of the same size. Put each parchment paper square on top of a foil square and fold diagonally in half to form a triangle. Open up.

Divide the fruits into 4 and arrange each portion in the center of each opened square—remember that you will be serving the fruit in the envelopes, so arrange the fruit neatly.

Add a vanilla bean half, a cinnamon stick half, a star anise, a bay leaf, and 1 tbsp orange juice to each triangle.

Close each triangle over the mixture, fold in the corners, and crumple the edges together to form airtight triangular bags.

Transfer the bags to a baking sheet and bake in the oven for 10–12 minutes, or until they puff up with steam.

To serve, put each bag on a serving plate and snip open at the table so that you can enjoy all the wonderful aromas as they are opened.

Calories: 77   Fat: 0.5g   Sat Fat: 0.1g   Salt: 0g

Mango
Cheesecakes

SERVES 4

corn oil, for oiling

2 tbsp polyunsaturated spread

½ tsp ground ginger

⅝ cup rolled oats

1 large ripe mango, about
   1 lb 5 oz/600 g

1⅛ cups virtually fat-free
   Quark soft cheese

scant ½ cup medium-fat soft cheese

12 raspberries, to decorate (optional)

Line the bottom and sides of 4 x ⅔-cup ramekins with waxed paper and very lightly oil. Melt the spread in a small pan over low heat, remove from the heat, and stir in the ginger and oats. Mix thoroughly and let cool. Using a sharp knife, cut the mango lengthwise down either side of the thin central pit. Peel the flesh. Cut away any flesh from around the pit and peel. Cut the flesh into chunks and set aside 4 oz/115 g. Put the remaining mango flesh into a food processor or blender and process until smooth. Transfer to a small bowl.

Drain away any excess fluid from the cheeses and, using a fork or tablespoon, blend together in a bowl. Finely chop the reserved mango flesh and stir into the cheese mixture along with 1 tablespoon of the mango puree. Divide the cheesecake filling evenly between the ramekins and level with the back of a spoon. Cover each cheesecake evenly with the cooled oat mixture and let chill in the refrigerator for at least 3 hours for the filling to firm.

To serve, carefully trim the lining paper level with the oat mixture. Since the oat base is crumbly, place an individual serving plate on top of a ramekin when turning out the cheesecakes. Holding firmly, turn both over to invert. Carefully remove the ramekin and peel away the lining paper. Repeat for the remaining cheesecakes. Spoon the mango puree around each cheesecake and decorate the top of each with 3 raspberries, if using. Serve at once.

| Calories: 287 | Fat: 14.6g | Sat Fat: 7.2g | Salt: 0.3g |

Fruity Stuffed
Nectarines

SERVES 4

4 ripe but firm nectarines or peaches

5 oz/140 g blueberries

4 oz/115 g fresh raspberries

⅔ cup freshly squeezed orange juice

1–2 tsp honey, or to taste

1 tbsp brandy (optional)

scant 1 cup low-fat strained plain
  yogurt

1 tbsp finely grated orange rind

Preheat the oven to 350°F/180°C. Cut the nectarines in half and remove the pits then place in a shallow ovenproof dish.

Mix the blueberries and raspberries together in a bowl and use to fill the hollows left by the removal of the nectarine pits. Spoon any extra berries around the nectarines.

Mix together the orange juice, honey, and brandy, if using, in a small bowl and pour over the fruit. Blend the yogurt with the grated orange rind in another bowl and let chill in the refrigerator until required.

Bake the berry-filled nectarines for 10 minutes, or until the fruit is hot. Serve with the orange-flavored yogurt.

Calories: 145   Fat: 0.5g   Sat Fat: 0g   Salt: 0g

Orange
Cups

SERVES 4

4 large oranges

1 cup buttermilk or low-fat plain
  yogurt

1 tsp honey

1 tsp chocolate shavings (optional)

Set the freezer to rapid freeze at least 2 hours before freezing. To ensure that the oranges stand upright, cut a thin slice from the base of each. Cut a lid from each orange at the other end and set aside. Carefully cut down the inside of each orange and remove the pith and flesh from each. Do this over a bowl to catch all the juice.

Discard the pith from the scooped out flesh, then chop the flesh to make a chunky puree. Place in a bowl with the juice. Stir in the buttermilk and the honey, and pour into a freezerproof container. Freeze for 1 hour. Place the empty orange shells upside down on paper towels and let drain.

Remove the orange mixture from the freezer and stir well, breaking up any ice crystals. Return to the freezer for an additional 30 minutes, or until semifrozen.

Stir again and use to fill the orange shells. Stand the filled oranges upright in a container. Freeze for an additional hour, or until frozen.

Before serving, transfer to the refrigerator for 30 minutes to soften slightly. Serve decorated with chocolate shavings, if using.

Calories: 88   Fat: 0.8g   Sat Fat: 0.4g   Salt: 0.1g